POEMS FROM THE BUDDHA'S FOOTPRINT

Translated into English Verse
from the Thai of *Sunthorn Phu*
by
Noh Anothai

Singing Bone Press
2017

ACKNOWLEDGMENTS

This translation of Sunthorn Phu's Nirat Phra Baht, these Poems from the Buddha's Footprint, is indebted to the Masters in Writing program at Lindenwood University in St. Charles, Missouri, whose director, Beth Mead, fostered an atmosphere where I could pursue my interests in translation. It also owes itself to the careful readership of Dr. Michael Castro, St. Louis's first poet laureate, whose affinity with Eastern religion and experience as a translator made him ideally suited to mentoring such a work. Much thanks to both of you. Portions of the manuscript were also presented at the Siam Society and Chulalongkorn University's Center for Translation Studies in June 2016.

Finally, I'd like to thank the editors and staff of the following journals for publishing these poems in earlier forms:

Asymptote: "Aubade with Elephants," "Antics on Elephant-back"
"Remembering Love Scenes at Pleasant River"
Structo: "Part & Cross"
Reunion: the Dallas Review: "Celebrations and Silence at the Buddha'sFootprint"
RHINO: "Inside the Cave-that-is-Screened"

Cover by Wady Alejandro Guzman

ISBN-10: 0-933439-12-1
ISBN-13: 978-0-933439-12-2

Library of Congress Control Number 2017939859

Published by Singing Bone Press
www.singingbonepress.com

PRAISE FOR POEMS FROM THE BUDDHA' S FOOTPRINT

A fine translation of Sunthorn Phu, for whom a pilgrimage was not so much holy as absurd, satiric, overburdened, and unwanted. The poem, a nirat, details a journey by boat and royal elephant through folkloric and dangerous landscapes by a grieving lover. It is also very funny. Noh Anothai's commentary is scholarly and wry, pointing out subversive puns, weird place names, and spirits that populate the countryside. His translation reads like a string quartet's performance of Thailand's great national poet.

　　—Andrew Schellig, *Bright as an Autumn Moon: Fifty Poems from the Sanskrit*

Few have attempted to translate Thailand's classical poetry, and even fewer have succeeded as Noh Anothai has in bringing Sun- thorn Phu's Poems from the Buddha's Footprint into English. Phu's is the definitive account of the time-honored pilgrimage to this holy site, but not even Montri Umavijani, his most prolific translator, completed a full-length version of it. Now, with his ear for Phu's subtle humor, witty wordplay, and changes in tone, Anothai braves the terrain of the untranslatable by creatively fusing various tech- niques while suggesting the movement and easy formality of Phu's poetry like no translator has done before. With this necessary addi- tion to the availability of Thai literature in English, this translation promises to launch our national poet among the great poets of the world.

　　—Dr. Phrae Chittiphalangsri, Department of Comparative Literature, Chulalongkorn University

Forward

Almost ninety miles north of Bangkok lies Wat Phra Phutthabaht, the Temple of the Buddha's Footprint. In February 1807, four days before the Magha Puja holiday, members of Bangkok's royal courts set out on pilgrimage for the Footprint, an annual tradition already two centuries old in their time. Among them were high-ranking court officials, sons of the royal family ordained as Buddhist monks, and even a host of palace women hilariously unsuited for the wilderness. Although today the trip takes less than three hours by car, for these pilgrims the Footprint lay three days ahead: the first two by boat, the third on elephant-back.

This motley procession may have been lost to us had it not included in its lower ranks a 21-year old page named Phu (pronounced "pooh"). Although today he is remembered as Sunthorn Phu, Phu the Eloquent, Thailand's national poet, at the time he was merely a prince's servant facing the dissolution of his first marriage. For reasons that we can only speculate about, his wife had not spoken to him for over a month, and Phu was called away without their having reconciled. Chan was her name, "moon," and images of moon-gazing, a standard of romantic poetry the world over, fill the poem that Phu wrote in his absence from her.

Phu's poem is a *nirat*, a uniquely Thai sort of verse travel memoir, of which Phu is the acknowledged master: accounts of journeys taken away from, and addressed to, a lover. In addition to straightforward travel narrative, there is in *nirat* poems a constant wordplay or metaphor-making that relates the names and features of the landscape, both natural and manmade, to thoughts of the beloved. In this way, *nirat* poems transcend the specificities of particular locales to map both physical locations and the topography of the heart.

Altogether, Phu's *Poems from the Buddha's Footprint* offer a rare and intimate glimpse into an age bygone today and sequestered in its own time: a royal procession out of Bangkok, then still a young capital, past the ruined city of Ayutthaya, and into the hills and caves around Thailand's most fabled place of worship—as well as into the private life of Thailand's greatest poet.

Common Thai Words Used in This Translation

Bang: a riverside village, like Bangkok

Khlong: a canal

Koh: an island

Pho: *Ficus religiosa,* a species of fig tree with heart-shaped leaves, under one of which the Buddha gained Enlightenment. When you see Pho trees, think of shade, shelter, and protection.

Sala: an open-air pavilion used as a rest stop by wayfarers or erected and embellished for ceremonial purposes

Wat: both temple and monastery, a walled compound consisting of several buildings including monk's quarters and others used for worship and religious functions

Contents

DAY ONE:
BANGKOK-AYUTTHAYA

Prologue

How many times I felt as if my chest might burst
or like an arrowhead were lodged inside my heart;
and for my lovely Moon, how I was set aflame. — *Chan*

For ever since the Second Month, you nursed
a grudge against me—and then, in the Third,
the lord I serve, who bears the lofty name,

away from his cloisters left on a rough journey
for which I, as a servant at his feet,
was parted from you, though most cherished by me,

until the royal progress was complete:
traversing the wilderness in pilgrimage
to worship the Footprint of the great Sage.

dual impulse = pilgrimage + compulsion

Part & Cross

The morning that I left you was the twelfth
the moon had grown. As daybreak drew close,
from pier and landing we hurried off.

I tried glimpsing the moon in between rows
of homes drifting by, but those places where
once I had seen you lay still and dark now

and this served to deepen my despair. –
On reaching Part, where a canal is set
crosswise with the river, I throbbed even more:

whoever thought such a name would be fit
for a village? As if they meant to say
here lovers are parted, never to meet!

From canal and village we rowed away
as from the palms, also called "parts," that grew there—
even those rose to meet me on my way!

Looking back at the Palace, I thought of my fair
and so raised my hands with my palms pressed,
addressing the gods of the court with this prayer:

"To you, my two fathers and wife I entrust.
In the following days, may no danger come nigh,
and may any man wishing to win her be curst

with death outright. So may it please the gods on high!"

5

Phu leaves just before dawn on Monday, February 8th, 1807, or "the twelfth/the moon had grown." According to the old lunar calendar, a month began on the new moon, "rose" for about two weeks as the moon waxed, then "fell" for another two. Though not named here, his starting point is the Temple of the Bell, where his master, Prince Pathamavamsa ("who bears the lofty name" in the Prologue), is ordained as a monk.

Immediately upriver, Phu passes Bang Chak, the village of *chak* or nipa palms, *Nypa fruticans*. But *chak* sounds like the verb "to leave, to be separated from," and the poet muses on the inauspiciousness of the name. (To this day, it's considered bad luck for couples to register their marriage licenses in Bang Chak.)

Phu notes Bang Chak Canal, which he would have seen on his left, and calls it "cross canal" because it would have been perpendicular to his course on the river, and because the word "cross" in Thai, as in English, suggests an obstruction. One thinks of Hermia in *A Midsummer Night's Dream:* "If then true lovers have been ever crossed,/it stands as an edict in destiny...a customary cross." With one last look at the city and its palaces, Phu makes a prayer for the wellbeing of his "two fathers" (understood as his and Chan's) and for the steadfastness of his wife.

The Town of Three-hundred Thousand

At Three-Sen I learned that, once, those grounds
were called "Three-*Saen*" throughout the city wide,
after the three hundred thousand who crowded round

to see the wonder drifting on the tide:
a Buddha all of bronze. They couldn't pull
its tonnage onto shore no matter how they tried,

and so they chose the bend "Three-Saen" to call,
which city-folk have named "Three-Sen" thereafter.
Then couldn't Love to fluctuation fall,

if even the words we use for places alter?
May the lady for whom my love is pure
like that brazen image never waver

though one-*saen* men should come, each coaxing her
with one-*saen* vows—yet may her heart remain sure.

§

When Phu passes Three-Sen, he recalls a legend about the naming of the village: once upon a time, three Buddha images (or by some accounts five) cast in solid bronze floated from the northern provinces into Bangkok. No matter how the townsfolk along the way tried to dredge these images from the water, they wouldn't budge until they reached their own desired destinations. Change the vowel sound and *saen* (a unit of one hundred thousand) becomes *sen*, a word of no meaning.

Chapel Home & Dear Market

Where the waters whirled on the outskirts of town,
I looked, but could see the palace no more,
a place as Chapel Home and Dear Market known,

though I had left both my home *and* my dear.
The orchards had reached the hour of bloom
and fruit trees towered above either shore:

Bananas with snake fruit and mango plums,
heavy with dewfall, hung in wet clusters.
Thronging the moon-wood's fruit, wrapped in perfume,

as if possessive of them, the bees hovered.
With you the yellow moon-wood shares a name
and seeing those trees, the heart in me shuddered.

Like me were the bees that clung about them,
the way that, once, I clung close to your side:
I paused, dwelling on this, and the tears came.

The love tree alone I saw its leaves shed,
like you shed your love for me out of anger.
The dewfall was I, who had wheeled and plead,

dropping moist words to cool your rancor.
Oh, if the love tree shed grudges instead,
then you wouldn't be angry at me much longer.

§

The city gives way to orchards when Phu reaches the northern outskirts of Bangkok, and enters rough terrain for the translator. In standard *nirat* mode, Phu puns on the names of what he sees beside the riverbank. There is the sandalwood tree, called *chan* in Thai, which sounds like his wife's name (in this translation the "moon-wood" tree, the most seamless alternative); the bees around them, *phu*, which sounds like the poet's own name; and the white or lavender *rak* blossom, which sounds like the word for "love."

Through the Ladies' Midst

Whole stretches of piers lined the riverside
at Kwan Market, near the Sandalwood Manor.
Beside the covered landing on my right

were boats crowded parallel with one another,
and what a clamor the merchants in them raised.
They looked rather pretty, those shop-mothers:

so snug were the shirts in which they dressed
I gazed at those garments with a sigh
as we went rowing through the ladies' midst.

As the hour grew late, the sun bleached the sky;
we reached Pak Kret, where we rested the oars
and, all at ease, took our meal straightaway;

then, with our strength renewed, set out once more.
The men were livelier now and loquacious grown
so that, at Spoke Village, near the Sand Bar,

were speaking all at once, while I alone
wondered: *What if this were "Spook," village of spirits?*
Someone, call the ghouls and goblins over to listen:

to them may I entrust my one and dearest
so he who dares court her gain no profit!

11

§

As Phu passes Kwan Market, he sees a floating market, once an ordinary sight along central Thailand's canals and waterways, but now mostly tourist destinations. The reader should not think too much about Phu's candid assessment of the female merchants working the market; while the poem is ostensibly addressed to his wife, it is also a public work. The women would have been hawking fruits and vegetables or cooking simple meals on small stoves inside their boats.

Phu only mentions Pak Kret, a pronounced bend around an island in the river, as the place where he and his companions break for lunch. The poet is more interested in the etymology of Phud Village—is it *phud,* the Thai verb "to speak," or does it come from the Indic word *bhuta,* a "ghost" or "ghoul"? The adjacent "sand bar" was a navigational hazard in times of low water during Phu's day.

The Mon Women

At Crownton, with such pain was I pierced through:
I had to leave in service of the Crown.
My heart sank deeper as I thought of you

then, when our prows drew close to Thatching-town,
I urged the men to row harder until
we reached Three Hills, where such a blaze poured down

that each of us grew faint and weak of will.
There I saw Mons come by the shoreside, dressed
in sarongs that rippled down to their heels,

but through a slit, each time a foot was raised,
the calves beneath flashed white before our eyes—
whoever sees such women would be pleased.

Their houses, too, they built unlike us Thais:
above the roofs were wide, but small the space below
like they were used for holding a family's rites.

Their neighborhood lay stretched in one long row,
which I saw portside only, passing through.

13

§

This passage attests to the ethnic diversity of the Chao Phraya River Basin. Historically, the river flowed through the village of Krasaeng, cutting it in half (the name refers to a cover for boats woven out of thatch, hence the translation). On the east bank was Krasaeng-Thai, a typical Thai village, while the other was Krasaeng-Mon. The Mon kingdoms once dominated much of central Thailand and lower Burma, where the Mon people are still a major part of the population.

The Wind After Lunch

At Wat Tamnak, we paused just long enough
to have our lunch, then in the ebb and flow
dipping the oars, once more set off.

The water at that time of day was low.
Even rivers have a time they must recede,
but as for my sufferings—not so,

because the jungle still lay far ahead,
through which we'd have to trek after the river,
and then my body would suffer indeed!

The wind sighed hard. I wished it would deliver
a message to her, my one-hundred *chang:*
not to be false, but preserve her honor.
For her alone, my heart rose in a pang.

15

§

The shell of Wat Tamnak's 600-year old ordination hall, where Phu and his men stop for lunch, crumbles near the Chao Phraya River today. In this passage—which mainly foreshadows the ride through the forest to come—Phu calls his wife, his fortune: his "one hundred *chang*," an old form of currency equivalent to roughly two thousand dollars today.

The Bare-Headed Bird

The wind that was sighing died down somewhat
at Buffalo, on the fields where herds graze.
Continuing north, we next reached a spot

where the river went its separate ways
around an island, splitting into two routes,
each one named by elders in ancient days:

the island called "Big," of homes destitute,
and the opposite bank called "Ratchakhram."
We skirted the first and kept it to port.

Oh, if a single current, if one stream,
can be obstructed by an island,
and two branches grow from a single stem,

then couldn't a lover grow double-minded?
Once we had put that island astern
the river flowed free, but at the next bend

once more in our course were we forced to turn:
where it broke, at Banyan, into three forks.
The land to the north was Si Kuk, I learned.

Here birds filled the sky and in great flocks
prowled the shallows for the fish that played there.
A white egret whisked one up with its beak

before flapping its wings into the air.
Headed downriver, there came bobbing past
a pelican, and I wondered: *To where?*

If, back to Bangkok, tell her I once pressed
close to myself how I'm longing for her.
—so I would have said, but he flew away first

to light by a stork in the purling water.
That bare-headed bird let out a squawk,
rippled his dewlap, and bristled his feathers.

For his flagrant head, men loathe such a stork,

17

and, seeing him there, the heart in me broke.

his afraid to be alone, old, and ugly

Phu makes much about the appearance of an island in the Chao Phraya and how the river splits "into two routes" around it. Though Koh Yai, the island in question, literally means "Big Island," in reality it is a tiny piece of land in the river opposite Ratchakhram municipality. The river indeed splits into two courses around the little island—but, no sooner done, merges into one again.

Phu's analogy is more appropriate a few miles farther north. At Bang Sai, village of banyan trees, the much smaller Noi River meets the Chao Phraya, which veers sharply to the east, forming a three-way intersection. Here, as is *de rigueur* in *nirat* poems, Phu examines the avian life surrounding him. But whereas this appears in many poems as a rhetorical exercise—pairing birds and plants together based on the sound of their names and what they connote, rather than on what is true to nature—Phu gives an apparently straightforward account of the wildlife he encounters.

However, the final bird Phu describes also has metaphorical significance: the lesser adjutant stork (*Leptoptilos javanicus*). An unsightly bird, the stork has a bare neck and head with a fringe of hair-like feathers that gives the impression of baldness—a trait repugnant to Thais of the past. Phu may have been thinking of the main antagonist in the folk-epic *Khun Chang Khun Phaen*—the standard version of which he would help compose in the court of King Rama II. In that story, the villain's mother dreams of a lesser adjutant stork before Chang's birth; he is subsequently born bald. Khun Chang grows into a crass, overweight man. Throughout the epic he tries to win the hero's wife while the man is away. No wonder the stork's appearance unnerves Phu. Throughout this *nirat*, Phu is anxious about other men courting his wife, of which the bird is symbolic.

Rose Island & the Summer Palace

At Rose Island, an island arose mid-river—
just as arose this business of state,
from whence rose the woes in my heart's center:

dredging them from my chest would be a feat
greater than dredging the land from the flood.
So, lost in my cares and bearing their weight,

to follow the river, onward I rowed.
A moment later, In's Island appeared.
Now, I can't say if this is a falsehood,

but from old accounts, I have long heard
that on this island a palace once stood
where ancient kings brought their wives to watch birds,

though abandoned today and left for the wood.
I looked and tried the truth to ascertain—
it seemed the reports were true indeed.

But where buildings once stood, dry timber leans;
crocodiles and crooks have the place as their lair.
If you had come with, you'd ask me to explain

all the things seen at the riverside here.

20

§

The "old accounts" Phu heard were correct: since the seventeenth century, Bang Pa In (called in Phu's day "Bang Koh In," the island village of In) was the site of a royal holiday retreat. By Phu's time, however, it had long stood abandoned. It was not until the reign of King Rama IV, towards the end of Phu's life, that reconstruction began. But it was King Rama IV's son, the cosmopolitan King Chulalongkorn, who ultimately transformed Bang Pa In into a magnificent summer residence with gardens, ponds, throne halls, government offices, and manors built in Thai, Chinese, and European styles. So it remains today, a premier tourist attraction and easy day-trip from Bangkok, thronged with double-decker buses and visitors snapping photographs. Such is the nature of change and impermanence!

Shortcut to the Old Capital

We past Monk's Island and those waters where junks
met with disaster in days of old. *Can religion save him?*
But Hurt Island was where my heart truly sank

for, by my comrades-at-oars, I was told
that tigers used the next bend as a ford.
I looked for tigers, but no tigers beheld;

if I had, I would have leapt overboard
and given my pitiful self as their prey.
So, still in one piece, our navy entered

the canal called Takian—to my dismay,
because in this *khlong* the only tongue heard
was of Muslim settlers speaking Malay.

One wouldn't be pleased with how they appeared; *his, like cool ok*
I kept my face turned for they seemed so uncouth *but not doing anything*
as my friends from the fleet hollered and jeered *to stop them*

until at last we reached the canal's mouth.

Phu and his boat-mates draw near the old capital of Ayutthaya and pass two more minor islands before taking a shortcut to the ruined island-city. The canal, Khlong Takian (a type of tree, *Hopea odorata*), is home to a neighborhood of *khaek*—a term Thais apply broadly to people of Middle Eastern, South Asian, and Malay/Indonesian descent based on perceived physical and religious similarities. These, Phu says, came from *Tani,* short for Pattani, a Malay sultanate far to the south. Pattani was a vassal state of Ayutthaya through the 15th century, so it's not surprising that Phu encounters their descendants near the old city.

Phu's description of the *khaek* is unflattering, but at least the poet (who consistently portrays himself as more reserved and socially-awkward than the other men) doesn't take part as his friends heckle them.

A Roost for Crows

I saw monasteries along the river,
but their state was more somber than I can record:
Stupas and sermon halls were falling over;

the rooms where monks quartered, falling apart.
At the sight of Wat Dharma, my heart quailed
for, even though the Hind Palace's lord

in his faith had had those cloisters rebuilt
from ruins into a temple that shone—
that temple is still "Dha-r-ma" called.

So I'd be "dha-r-mented," though a gold crown
were granted to me, and a belt at my waist;
as you, to your grudge against me, would cling on.

I feared for our future as we rowed past.
Then, at Lotus Canal, I was filled with awe
as from our streaming procession I gazed

at what remained of great Ayutthaya.
Its palaces, both Front and Hind, lie interred
within the silence of the jungle now,

broken only by the lonesome crying of birds;
their crumbling spires a roost for crows;
and this once-peopled city, a graveyard.

§

Between the 14th-18th centuries, the empire of Ayutthaya dominated much of mainland Southeast Asia. Situated on an island at the confluence of three rivers, it had access to the Gulf of Thailand and the sea routes beyond, making Ayutthaya a center for global commerce. It exchanged embassies with courts as far away as Versailles, and the cosmopolitan city boasted thriving expatriate communities, who described Ayutthaya as more populous and opulent than either London or Paris. Despite weathering previous attempts to conquer it, the city fell to Burmese forces in April 1767 after a fourteen-month siege. Buildings were set to flame, temples looted, and Ayutthaya's people, noble and common alike, killed or forced to march to Burma as prisoners of war.

When Phu leaves Takian Canal, he comes upon the island-city and its ruins. Conspicuous is one temple, Wat Dharma. Burmese forces held this monastery each time they laid siege on Ayutthaya, razing it when they finally sacked the town. Perhaps because of its symbolic importance, the "Hind Palace's lord" had the *wat* rebuilt in 1785.

Phu spins a convoluted analogy based on the pronunciation of the *wat*'s name. The Thai word for the Buddha's teaching, his Dharma, is usually pronounced with a short initial vowel and no *r*—"Dhamma," its Pali pronunciation. But the name of this *wat* uses the Sanskrit long *a*, plus the *r* sound—"Dha-r-ma"— making it sound like the word "to-r-ma," cognate English "torture, torment," both related to Latin *tortura*. Phu says that the temple, though restored by its royal patron, nevertheless keeps an inauspicious name. Likewise, he claims that he would be unable to shake off his toubles were he given a gold crown and belt, signs of royal favor. Likewise, neither would his wife give up her grudges against him.

Elegy for the Old Capital

Oh, impermanent:
a city of its monarchs overthrown,
subdued by war, then by the silent wood.
If people still inhabited the town

then every quarter would be ringing loud
with pipes and drums, assembled instruments,
and conch-horns blaring high above the crowds.

Now one can only think of transience,
hearing nothing but the cries of birds.
Then, too, with brush the city's streets are dense,

its fortunes fallen to both flame and sword.
But by my grandparents have I been told
that, once before, Ayutthaya prospered

under a line of rulers who upheld
the world, and very source of woe allayed.
Now, looking at its remnants, how I felt

it was a shame I had been born too late.
Through walls as high as these, and moats as deep
how could the Burmese forces penetrate

and fierce into the inner city sweep
as if no men were left it in this last
ordeal? Or had the city spent its final troop

that they could come and slaughter as they pleased,
like nothing in this world were easier?
Then for my wife with worry was I seized:

Outside, to me your heart's defense seems sure
just like the walls of our old capital.
But I have never seen into its true center—

what if men broke into that citadel?
Therefore I raised this prayer to the heavens:
may your heart be unlike the town that fell,

but like our kingdom standing in the present,
steadfast and fearful not of anyone.
This way, ages from now, our love remains.

27

§

"Anicha" begins Phu's elegy for the fallen city of Ayutthaya. Usually translated–"alas," it is in fact short for *Anicha vata sankhara!*, a Pali phrase in Theravada Buddhist countries that announces the deaths of loved ones: Impermanent are all created things! To exclaim "Anicha!" is to express dismay for *lacrimae rerum,* the ephemerality of the world. Phu extends the Buddhist concept of impermanence, evident in the rise and fall of empires, to the human heart: the most fleeting thing of all.

At Our Lady of Joys

As sunset drew the evening to a close,
beside a monastery we rested the fleet,
a temple called Our Lady of Joys.

He helped me my sorrows to forget
—whoever it was who chose that name,
and has my thanks for it—nor do I kid.

We oarsmen and our masters, all who came,
debarked to boil rice or fetch firewood,
but I, choked up at having come so far from home,

heaved a giant sigh at the sight of food.
A mere handful of rice I had to force
myself to eat, which once I'd chewed

grated my throat. Water itself felt coarse,
and salty and sour alike tasted bitter.
I only ate to keep my gut from going hoarse.

And so, once darkness fell, dripping moisture,
we made our camp outside Our Lady of Joys
where I could only my lady remember.

Both masters and servants lay down to repose
upon the sandbank, but aboard his ship,
its curtains on all four sides drawn close,

he who was born of the gods went to sleep
until, late after the first gong, he emerged
to gave word for us to resume our trip.

§

By sunset on the first day, Phu has rowed with the royal corps for some ten or eleven hours. They stop for the night at Wat Mae Nang Pluem, an ancient temple on the northern side of the island-city. A Dutch account from 1640 recalls a legend about the temple's founding: Mae Nang Pluem ("the woman Pleum"), an old lady who lived on the site, unwittingly received King Naresuan (r. 1590-1604) into her home one stormy night. The King honored her by moving her into the Palace and constructing a monastery where her house stood. But *pleum* literally means "pleasure, delight," and the temple's name can be construed as "Wat of the Joyous Woman," which earns Phu's sarcasm. The next morning, the company resumes its journey "late after the first gong," perhaps around half past six a.m.

DAY TWO:
AYUTTHAYA-LANDING

A Ride to Landing

We left through a channel called Levee's Head,
whose banks, leading to Burma, were overrun
and crumbling—like me, from whom Love had levied

so heavy a toll and collected in groans.
Rounding the bend, where the grass was cropped short
along the shoreside at Oxcart Junction,

I scanned both directions in search of a cart,
thinking a ride to Landing I'd hire,
but bearing the burden of a broken heart

some six or seven oxcarts would require.
Our boat with that burden I had to fill,
with each oar-stroke mingling pain with desire.

Were there a bail at Bailspring, I'd be well:
I'd have bailed from me the source of my pain,
but saw only jungle reach for the hills,

and then, at Pák-Chan, my chest throbbed again
for you and that village shared the same name,
which renewed my short-forgotten chagrin.

Next, to the village called Bidder we came,
led to that place by some pernicious star:
to reach, in bitterness of body, Bidder's homes,

and—ah, me!—that village stretched so far.
How could the townsfolk endure living there,
to Bidder-ness day and night grown familiar?

§

For the second leg of their journey, Phu and the royal fleet follow a tributary of the Pasak River northeast to Tha Reau, "Boat Landing." Phu's record of the second day's travels is disproportionately shorter than that of the first. He runs through a series of several locales and to most devotes hardly a line of characterization. For the rest, he spins analogies based on their names in typical *nirat*-mode. There is Levee's Head Channel, where I've punned on the words "levee" and "levy" (in the original Thai, Phu puns *ro*, "levee," with *ro*, "to wait for, to pine after"); Oxcart Junction, once an important meeting point for caravans; Pak-Chan (which recalls the name of Phu's wife, Chan); Bailspring; and Bidder, originally Bang Rakam, the village of snake fruit, whose name in Thai suggests "hardship." I have excised the most tedious lines.

Phu seems bored and uninspired here, and the reader is bored with him (the translator, too). But the poet doesn't nod for long: he'll make up for this with a colorful retelling his night in the woods and the bustle the following morning.

Arrival at Landing

When at last we reached Landing, the dockside stirred
with the bustling of men and barges packed close.

For us a troop was waiting as we moored
and we began the cargo to unload
(each man of his own things keeping best guard);

then on the bank waited in a great crowd
as, mounting the *sala* we'd raised in the river,
our lord disrobed where the clear water flowed.

When he was done, we raced into the river,
each man ecstatic to free from oars,
but still my feelings smoldered like a cinder

that no leisure in the water could restore.
Looking over the bank, my vision spun
nor could I keep my head raised anymore.

But in my hardship, like my own kin
a friend massaged my back and smoothed my shoulders,
and helped me feel somewhat better again.

Aubade with Elephants

When, over the vast jungle, daylight failed,
the elephant-handlers chose twenty beasts
and led them for outfitting in the field.

With silks they draped one whose walk wavered least
and as our master's own mount set her apart;
then in the same clearing laid down to rest

awaiting the dawn, when our march would start.
His Highness as well went straightway to bed
with troops arranged at four points to keep guard.

The other attendants slept as if dead,
utterly spent—all but myself, for so strong
was the heartache that my love for you bred

that I could hear the watchmen before long
taking their break, and their voices at play
challenging each other to compose half-songs.

Some sang of the woods as they do in the plays
in slow, plaintive tones. Though I could have joined,
instead, through the night I lay turned away

and gazed at the moon wheeling his course.
Reminded of you, by chance his namesake,
my pain was too great to be written in verse!

At that hour when the wild roosters break
the night's calm with their crowing, and the songbirds
start calling each other, I started awake—

thinking it was your clear voice that I heard;
but then saw the moon, still bright overhead,
the elephants in single-file ordered.

My comrades also awoke, and these made
their own racket: some hollered to rouse
the stragglers; rolled matts or rations bundled,

or bickered over whose howdah was whose.

Some others clambered onto elephant-back:
to them, piece by piece, our equipment arose

but when they couldn't keep up, then *crack!*
went the dishes; plates clanged against cups;
rice pots were shattered; bowls and pitchers broke,

and chili-paste urns lay bottom-side up
wherever they fell. But we only tied
the trays of betelwood to strands of rope

and left them hanging from the elephants' sides—
in trying times lovelier than earthenwares.
The women who came made a pitiful sight:

their baubles were broken, their combs and mirrors,
their pots of creams and turmeric powder.
The owners could only watch this in tears.

Come time to board, they fared little better:
in trim, foot-length skirts so neatly dressed,
the girls were unable to swing their legs over

the elephants' humps. Instead, all distressed,
they'd flail on the cords around the animals' necks.
And if one of the elephants should twist

a trunk towards them, the maidens would shriek,
tear their Indian-print dresses, lose their grips,
and to the ground tumble with a great smack.

The officers chortled until their sides were stiff
—then, suddenly stern, called their men to make haste.
Onto the elephants some hauled themselves up

and pulled the women after them by their wrists;
while others, swapping modesty for speed,
heaved the poor girls aboard by the waist.

§

It would be tempting to compare Sunthorn Phu with Bashô, Japan's most celebrated poet, who two centuries earlier traveled the Japanese countryside writing poetry inspired by the landscape. But unlike Bashô, Phu is a reluctant outdoorsman; he prefers the comforts of the city to any forest sojourn. Thus, after nightfall, when the prince's watchmen begin playing "half-songs" with each other—a popular pastime in Phu's day, where one person or team composes a line of verse and another extemporizes a matching couplet—and "sing of the forest," a common mode in Thai poetry and drama, Phu turns aside, either from a sense of poetic superiority or from his own desire for sleep. Either way, his characterization of himself is delightfully petulant.

Antics on Elephant-back

Once sunlight across the landscape had spread,
and each man had eaten to his heart's fill,
His Highness, throned on the mount of state, bid

his driver lead us into the hills.
Departing our campsite by the pier
we entered an expanse of open field,

our caravan kicking into the air
above the mountain-pass, enormous dust clouds,
each stride causing the howdahs to waver,

so that our bodies were jostled about.
Guard-elephants ringed His Highness' mount;
behind, in a long train, we servants rode.

Unlucky as always, I sat at the front
of a young bull, his head dripping with oil.
For laughs, a friend slapped my ride with his hand:

the creature charged for the woods, and I fell
—almost fell off, but the rider in rear
caught hold of me. *Can you picture my gall?*

I wanted to leap off that beast, right there
in the middle of that forsaken wood,
but knew I'd never live it down—my peers

all would have said I had a woman's heart.

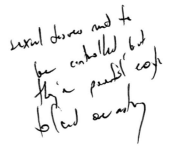

39

§

Male elephants go through periodic hormonal surges known scientifically as "musth" or "must," during which they are particularly aggressive and irritable. At these times, their temporal glands secrete a thick, oily substance called temporin, which runs down their heads. It's on such a "young bull" that Phu rides, presenting his friends with the opportunity for fun at his expense. Phu says he rides "in front," or on the hump between the elephant's shoulders; there would have been a second rider over its hip.

DAY THREE & BEYOND:
THE TEMPLE OF THE BUDDHA'S FOOTPRINT

A Country Market

At Foxfire, we crossed the Elephant Bridge,
having come one hundred and fifty *sen*.
A grove of Pho trees cast a gentle shade

and no space beneath was empty of men.
On either roadside, they had their wares spread;
each, hawking at once, raised a commotion.

I steered my elephant close to one side,
saw items arranged, both savories and sweets,
but heard in the curries was stewed centipede

—nothing but anguish for city-goers to eat,
whether maidens or men. At this, my stomach turned,
and so my elephant in long strides I led

back down the road. Dust-clouds were driven on the wind
as birds with their wailing filled the dense wood.
I felt it inside me: the cuckoos mourned

and pheasants crooned like Javanese flutes.

§

The distance from Landing to the Buddha's Footprint is a mere twelve miles, which Phu reckons in terms of *sen* (literally "lines") or units of forty meters— a total of 475 *sen* in all. The existence of an ancient road leading to the Temple attests to its importance as a pilgrimage site; King Songtham, in whose reign the Footprint was discovered, enlisted Dutch laborers to construct the road. Colloquially, it was called the "road of white men looking through lenses," a nod to the new leveling instruments these Europeans used.

Now on the final leg of his journey, the places Phu names are *sala*, roadside shelters, a bridge for elephants to cross (now built for modern traffic), and *bo*, pools of fresh water dug by subsequent monarchs for use by pilgrims.

Woe's Well

We next made our way towards the well called Woe:
in my hardship, this name grated my ear.
Even if the well's name I didn't know,

the sight of the well was enough cause for despair.
A level path led into the jungle's midst:
after two-fifty *sen,* the herd lumbered near

that deep reservoir, and as we strode past
I urged my elephant into a canter
so that Woe's Well into the thickets was lost,

although my spirit couldn't struggle from under
its woe. A marsh at Nong Khonti we found,
that was all mud, tall grass, and black water.

Elephants had left in the soggy ground
along its banks, their feet's impressions,
so the ground, like my heart, was pock-marked with wounds

brimming with water as dark as the fen's.
At that murky water I gazed in dismay
and hurried after the other elephants.

I reckoned how many *sen* I'd come on my way
at over some fifty and three-hundred.
Oh, even these distances fell away

—then why couldn't my heartache also be shed?
On the right I was confronted by the green wood;
on the left, by a range of foothills met.

§

The next two sites Phu notes are water sources, one manmade and one natural. The former was built in 1633 beside a grove of *ashok* trees, called simply *sok* in Thai. While the word *ashok* comes from Indic roots and means "sorrow-less," the shortened form in Thai means simply "sorrow." Thus, when Phu passes the "*sok* well," he construes it as "the well of sorrow, the well from which sorrow is drawn." After Woe's Well, Phu encounters the marsh Nong Khonti ("nong" means marsh or swamp).

The Idols at Fallen Hill

We next reached the *sala* at Monk's Shelter:
A riot of trees grew on the grounds there.
In the forests beyond lurked bandits and tigers;

—one can't come and go without taking care.
But I don't find tigers fearful when heart-sore
and scanned the slopes above for their lair.

Reaching the four-hundred mark and no more,
the command was given to pick up our speed
because we neared the elephants' feeding hour.

Our prince's elephant was so hurried
that sweat was streaming down its reddened face.
At Yaw Pool, we waited for the tuskers to feed

as well as the other troops to catch up with us.
In the meantime, to Fallen Hill I made
my way to revere its holy images.

Before those idols I lit candles and prayed
that in the jungle's lap they'd keep us safe.
The Hill looks like it was left by a cascade

of falling boulders—oh, how like myself!
Fallen in hardship since leaving your side
first for the jungle, and then for this shrine by the cliff.

I fought back my tears, my mind unsettled
and knowing no respite from my love.
At last, a goodbye to the spirits I bid,

saying, "May you be well; my time's come to go."
When His Highness was ready to proceed
from the Pool, in a sprawling train we drove

the elephants forth, single-file beneath
the vertical glare of the day-making sun
with our master himself throned in the lead.

About that time the gongs are struck at one

47

we reached the monastery, which was already full
of people; dismounted, and brought our gear down

from the elephants beside that sacred hill.
The abbot welcomed our lord and invited
him into his comfortable, wood-paneled cell,

where blissfully he joined his brotherhood.
Huddled outside, officers and servants alike
sheared fronds for shelter over our heads.

His need to
accept Buddhism

§

After passing Monk's Shelter, Phu's caravan arrives in the vicinity of the Buddha's Footprint. Phu has the chance to first visit an adjacent shrine at Fallen Hill—so called because the Hill looks like an enormous pile of individual boulders dumped into place. On its slopes is a shrine to the Hill's guardian genii.

Celebrations & Silence at the Buddha's Footprint

When evening came and drew night's darkness down,
one could not hear above the horns and shells;
the blare of pipes; gongs, drums, and xylophones;

the endless ringing of the temple bells.
How was it that the drumbeats and the din
could captivate me so, and make me thrill?

From every corner rose the noise of men.
Outside, the trees were gilded with moon-glow;
the monks' recital of the great Questions

reverberated down the slopes below.
Since now it was his splendid mid-month night,
the moon adorned himself with a halo.

The rocky nooks around the shrine shone bright
with lanterns, each one glowing like the moon;
and blossom-shaped candles dazzled my sight,

their wicks lit and flickering on the white stone,
as on the chapel's topmost spire,
on gable and finial, the moonlight shone.

Birds fled their roosts before the flowers of fire
that blossomed into sparks in the night air
and made the farthest reaches of the jungle thunder

such as no flowers on earth's surface can compare.
Fair-goers milled about the grounds until
behind a cloud, night's master led the stars.

Then, when the last voice died and bells fell still,
we made our camp along the mountain's slopes.
In that dismal hour, we were miserable,

bedding down amid the gleaming drops
of dew. Not only in the dark and chill
did we lie drenched, skin breaking into bumps,

the rock on which we lay was cold as well!

Thus we weathered the night, wind-cold and wet-cold,
yet all other coldnesses are bearable

except those of the heart. How difficult
these are, and most: sleeping far from your side.
Not piles of blankets, fold under fold,

could warm like holding you, the city's pride.
With my heart aching, I slept in the gloom
until, to signal the dawn, each rooster vied.

Some solace reached me while my senses were dim,
and I lay enwrapped in slumber's warm haze,
but no sooner come, then crumpled the dream

I had of dozing fast in your embrace
just as I did when we were still living
at peace in your home in happier days.

A short reprieve; then suddenly morning,
and I with a jolt awoke to the sound
of all the temple bells at once tolling.

Frantic for you, I reached a hand around
and clutched at nothing. My hurt knew no bounds.

§

There is at least a four-hour gap in Phu's narrative: between one o'clock, when the royal procession arrives at the Footprint, and sunset, when the night's festivities begin. Undoubtedly some of the pages doubled as musicians in the events described or orchestrated the fireworks; the palace women were probably in sole charge of flower arrangements. However, we don't know what hand Phu directly had in all of this. But like elsewhere when the poet nods, Phu compensates with a passage of particular accomplishment.

The Temple of the Buddha's Footprint

As the morning, but not my mood, grew brighter, *oof*
from our rations I made a quick breakfast;
chose joss sticks for worship, plus a taper,

then over the dew-covered lawns, I crossed.
The shade of Pho trees hung thick on the place
and flowering trees raised a cover against

the rising sun, granting such blissful ease
that men and women crowded in their shelter.
At the portal before the *naga* staircase

a pair of *rakshasa*, two giant ogres,
were standing guard, grimacing on either side,
baring their eyes and fangs like living creatures.

The serpents of the *naga* balustrade
seemed poised as well to coil and slither,
both forking their tongues and glaring ahead

though carved out of stone. In the shade under
a rain-of-gold tree that bloomed in the yard,
alms were being strewn: pieces of silver

stuffed inside betel. Of these, folk fought to hoard
as much as they could, snatching whole handfuls,
or over the piles of cowrie shells[1] clamored.

At the western slope, under the chapel,
ascetics of stone flashed white, toothy grins,
in tiger hides draped, wearing headdresses tall,

wispy whiskers on cheeks, beards on their chins.
There also, flanking the same stairwell,
as if ready to pounce, crouched two lions, twins—

---

1   As in other parts of the world, cowrie shells (*bia*) were long used as a form of currency in Siam. Today, the word for financial interest is *dok bia*, literally that which "sprouts" or "blooms" out of cowries.

admiring them, I climbed the steps to the chapel.
I merged with the crowd outside and with our palms pressed,
around the shrine we traced a right-wheeling circle[2],

and as we walked, on our surroundings gazed:
at wall-panels shimmering with glass pieces,
at columns on which glass mosaic blazed.

Their capitals were fashioned like lotuses
with leaves of gold layered up their height,
parted in the middle by mirror embosses.

Spanning the chapel's foundations, on every side
garuda stood grappling in their winged arms
with winding naga, serpentine in their might,

beside angels in greeting with conjoined palms.
Rows of golden finials, flawless in mold,
crowned the doorways' golden gable-frames.

Surmounting the shrine like that mountain called
the Yukhandhar[3], the temple's spire rose in tiers,
from their eaves dangling little bells of gold

with clappers like Pho leaves, which to hear
chiming above, through my heart sent a chill.
The massive panels of each chapel door

were inlaid entirely with mother-of-pearl
that contorted into arabesque designs.
Garuda and naga fought in the whorls;

and ogres clutched cudgels amid the vines,
whose winding tendrils hungry lions gnawed
and with angels at play were intertwined.

---

2   Daksina ("right," compare Latin "dexterous"): a sort of walking meditation. For
auspicious occasions, the practice is for celebrants to walk three times, clockwise,
around a shrine, as Phu does here. Circling "sinister"—with the left hand to the
shrine—is reserved for funerals.

3   A mountain in Thai cosmology.

Enclosed inside one whorl, Jambuvan stood;
in another Sugriva[4] raised his sword;
on a *garuda* in flight, Vishnu rode;

upon his swan-throne Lord Brahma appeared;
and deathless Indra[5] flourishing his ring
upon his elephant-mount was in-figured.

Inside, all four chapel walls were glistening,
burnished so brilliantly with golden paint,
and underfoot, the floor was laid with silver tiling.

The lesser shrine that housed the Buddha's Print
on golden columns stood, topped by a golden spire,
upon the underside of which mirrors shined,

reflecting the glare of the candle-fires.
From joss and incense burning, sweet smoke rose,
exhaling fragrance through that golden chamber.

---

4   Chomphuphan...Sugriva: two generals in the monkey army of the *Ramayana*.

5   Vishnu...Brahma...Indra: Hindu deities portrayed on their animal "mounts"
    according to standard iconography.

§

After arriving at the Temple, Phu seems not to have any official duties, or at least doesn't record them, and by the next morning is free to sightsee. What follows is a detailed description of the temple grounds and main chapel by day—a passage which in Thai middle schools was once memorized by students for recitation.

The catalogue of specific decorative patterns and architectural features may seem tedious, but keep in the mind how inaccessible the Temple was for most of its history. That said, the passage is challenging for a translator; besides specialized terms for particular designs, it features a whole menagerie of mythical creatures imported from India and Hinduism. These include *garuda*, creatures half-man and half-eagle that prey on *naga*, serpent-like animals; *rakshasa*, beings similar to ogres; characters from the Hindu epic *Ramayana*, and even the high gods of Hinduism, incorporated into Thai cosmology as beings subservient to the Buddha.

I did not aim for a literal translation for most of the passage, but rather strove to evoke their affect: of opulence and extravagant artistry.

Phu's Prayer

From its right side, I approached the Footprint,
knelt, then touched my pressed palms to my forehead,
and three times to the floor before me, bent,

reflecting on the goodness of the deed:
"My reverence to the Footprint being done,
now may the Triple Gemstones[6] give me heed!

To poor karma in this lifetime was I born
and have so many shapes of hardship seen:
frustration and anger; a master's scorn;

my plans always thwarted; and meager my means!
May that word be far removed from me—"poor"—
if I in human form am born again;

Both jealous women and slinking whores,
may neither of these to my heart come close;
of men, may it never be my lot to fare

alongside those who by nature are false.
Whomever I love, may I win her as well—
oh, may the good merit made aid me in this!

In the sum of my parts, may no sickness dwell,
and as Indra himself, let me be handsome.
On Father and Mother may no troubles fall,

nor to my relatives adversity come;
no word that wounds the heart should reach their ears
but may they dissolve before reaching them.

In peace may they live, and free from the fear
of fetters and rods; may they never feel
a hard master's hand or labor severe;

but he himself die who wishes them ill.

---

6   Triple Gemstones: that is, the Buddha, the Dharma (his teachings), and the
Sangha (the monkhood; more generally, the community of the faithful).

And may they all attain honor and rank."
Thus I prayed, then bid the Lord's Footprint farewell

to see the sights of the surrounding hills.

§

Before his death, the Buddha prescribed four places wherein his followers can go to reflect on his teachings: the sites of his birth, enlightenment, first sermon, and ultimate death and passing into Nirvana. With the spread of Buddhism and the rise of Buddhist art in subsequent centuries, monasteries came to assume this role as well—though, as the prayer Phu makes at the shrine reveals, more secular concerns often play a role in popular worship. Phu mostly concerns himself with living comfortably in this world with the hope for better future incarnations.

Phu's confession that he has "known a master's scorn" is usually understood as his having been jailed for courting Chan (see guide to reading at the end of this book).

An Unfortunate Encounter

I climbed my way up the Lankan Pho Hill
on which stood a grove of these Ceylonese trees
and a *sala* housing a line of bells

which they tolled until evening without pause.
A frangipan thicket shaded the peak
and from this a trail lead to monks' houses.

There was a cave, too, overhung in rock,
with splendid Buddha images inside.
To see these especially, people came in flocks,

just as I write it, both men-folk and maids.
The little Lord Novice, looking handsome,
with a servant behind him bearing his shade,

that selfsame morning happened to come;
but too late I saw him—and nearly died
leaping out of his path to avoid him,

hands flailing for a grip on the rock-side.
I caught hold of a branch by some miracle,
so the worst injury was done to my pride.

I had to take the long way down the hill
cutting through brush, deeply embarrassed.
There were some women when I reached the vale

who took one look and broke into jest
among themselves. I feigned indifference,
as if I weren't disheveled or hadn't noticed,

although my cheeks burned; and off I went.

§

Should we take this humorous episode as straightforward reportage or exaggeration for comic relief? It's plausible if we imagine Phu being completely absorbed by his surroundings, then perhaps rounding a corner directly into the Novice's path. Of course, Phu could not have fallen off a cliff, but perhaps tumbled down a sheer slope for a dozen feet.

A number of high-ranking government officials made the pilgrimage to the Buddha's Footprint. Besides Prince Pathamvamsa, there were other princes of higher rank who went along and who were also ordained as monks. According to one Thai historian, the "little Lord Novice" to whom Phu refers in this passage is one such prince. Six years younger than Phu, this prince would be appointed "Supreme Patriarch" of Thailand's Buddhist clergy in 1851: His Holiness Paramanuchit Chinarot.

If this is true, the unfortunate encounter they have is the first of many: in late middle-life, when Phu himself was ordained as a monk, he took orders at the temple where His Holiness was abbot. It's said that the two of them did not get along.

Cleft Hill

I wondered why the Cleft Hill was so-called,
and an elderly man unwound my suspense:
what time the king of giants (I was told)

seized Sita, who shone with beauty's brilliance,
and fled from her husband, fearing battle,
his chariot struck with force immense

the solid rock, which split beneath his wheel;
thus the landmark has been cleft ever since.
The color left me as I looked at the Hill

for, since departing for jungle and plain,
not once have I glimpsed my gentle Moon.
Will we, like the Hill, be cleft in twain?

Thus I wondered, then felt for footholds down
the hill-paths by swaying trees overgrown.

It should be obvious to anyone why Cleft Hill, a local landmark, is so-called: it looks like a clean blow sheared it in half. But Phu takes the opportunity to recall a local legend about its origin and, in doing so, demonstrates his knowledge of Thai literature.

In the Sanskrit epic *Ramayana* (c. 500-600 BCE), the giant king's abduction of Sita, Prince Rama's wife, ignites a war between their kingdoms. A testimony to the influence of Indic culture throughout Southeast Asia, local versions of the *Ramayana* abound in the region. In Thailand, where the epic is called the *Ramakien*, the tale has become so localized that several places have long been identified with the story—as here at Cleft Hill.

Inside the Cave-that-is-Screened

At the foot of one hill, we reached a cave
overhung by a massive slab of stone:
a fringe of bamboo grew beyond its eave

while the slope above was tangled and green
with profuse other plants. This the ancients
in bygone days dubbed the Cave-that-is-Screened.

There was a *sala* outside the entrance;
from here we invited six girls to go in
and explored the rooms hung with stone pendants

from which water was dripping like beads of rain.
When the candles went out and all forms were hid,
the maidens ran pell-mell into the men

and through the chamber their cries resounded.
And we, of course, through the darkness gave chase:
whoever could catch a girl as she fled

and fondle her body in his embrace,
that fellow with whiskers of clay was smeared.
Soon we were all mangy as alley cats.

When, into the sunlight, we reappeared,
we whooped and hollered to see our pals:
how we by the women had been disfigured!

Some bore on their arms long marks left by nails.
Still laughing, we left to see more of the hills.

§

In this passage, Phu is suddenly joined by five other men and an equal number of young women, on whom the former play a practical joke. The scene resembles one that occurs in the Thai court epic *Inao*, which Phu would have known: when the princess Busaba and her maidservants go worship an idol inside a cave, her lover Inao steals inside with them, extinguishes the torches, and then. . . .   O◡O

In Chalawan's Cavern

We next reached a cave called the Chalawan
and lovely was every corner and groove
of that massive cavern. The walls of stone

glimmered like starlight, streaked with the hues
of rain-purpled clouds, rubies, and emeralds.
We pretended that in its jags and eaves

the figures of animals lay concealed:
a red-eyed rabbit, like one from the wood,
some saw, while others only its body beheld,

and as we looked on, still others continued
claiming they saw just its throat or its head.
Looming above us, the shafts of stone stood

precarious, as if they would crush us all dead,
and yet up and down they gleamed through the black,
when by our candles they were illuminated.

Looking around me, I felt my chest ache
because you, my beloved, were not there,
so I invited my friends to turn back,

since there were still many rooms to explore.
I wanted to see what more shapes I could find,
but by then the sun was past his last hour.

We all returned to the Sage's Footprint.
How exhausted I was, was no joke;
again we slept cold, each sprawled out and spent;

until back to life in the morning I woke;
then, to see more of the sights, off I went.

§

The location of Chalawan Cave I couldn't determine, perhaps because it has since Phu's time collapsed on itself. Equally likely, however, is that this cavern—with fabulous walls "streaked with the hues/of rain-purpled clouds, rubies, and emeralds"—is pure fiction. Fantastic caves are common settings in Thai folklore; indeed, "Chalawan" is the name of a ferocious crocodile in one story who can shapeshift into a man, but dwells in a splendid, well-furnished grotto underwater.

While Skirting the Market

I peered a way's off and saw water gleaming,
and thought by skirting the market I would head over.
The makeshift stalls with produce were teeming. *she's prickly*

Seeing the porcupine quills, I missed my lover: *she's prickly*
how I would watch her unravel her hair.
Herbal teas, dried and crushed, and various other

healing plants the countryfolk were selling there:
pods and gourds with powdered seeds inside,
cure-alls through which the body's ills disappear.

Shameful alone seemed the *labee* seed:
what slave's son would sport a scalp so bald?
Who's bald should humble himself, but instead

these sat in plain view and for ten farthings sold!
I turned aside and drew close to a well
where a trail started, leveled by many footfalls.

Admiring the mountains, I followed this trail
between two low hills and down to a creek
with such sunlit and spotless water full

that on the creek-bed a man could count the rocks. *he yells*
Both men and women were there, washing together,
their voices rising in joy from the brook,

and, more troubling, among their worshippers
were monks splashing around and turning up foam.
I wished to be free from that place and their chatter

and thus made my way towards Pleasant Stream.

§

Phu once more explores the vicinity of the Buddha's Footprint, skirting the market where countryfolk are selling medicinal herbs and other traditional drugs. These include porcupine quills, reputed to have specials powers (and which, oddly enough, remind Phu of a woman's long hair), and smooth, polished *labee* seeds. As in the passage "The Bare-Headed Bird," Phu alludes to the crass, bald-headed antagonist of *Khun Chang Khun Phaen,* who courts the hero's wife in his absence.

Recalling Love Scenes by Pleasant River

A tree leaned its branches over the water.
I helped tie a vine-swing around one bough.
The ladies took turns at calling each other

to push them on this—but slowly now, slow.
Like Sita hanging herself in the theater,
the girls swaying each other seemed just so.

The vine, though, was brittle, and one girl, unluckier
than her companions: when she was swung,
the cord snapped and plunged her into the water;

her breast-cloth flew off, her gold trinkets rang.
In laughter both banks erupted as one
but at the sight of those women, a pang

rose in my chest, and I stifled a groan.
Still, that pleasant stream lived up to its name:
As in the *Inao*, the girls' worship done,

the gallant watched as they played in the stream,
one and the same seemed his story and mine.
The pebbles like crystal or the red gem

glimmered; or, if green, were brilliantly green;
there came little fish, two by two, swimming past,
and flower petals of all kinds were strewn

on the waters within the lovers' midst—
though heartsick, these flowers gave me some cheer.
Of these the couples competed to gather the most;

on this afternoon, more than a hundred pairs
to dip themselves in the stream had come down,
and steal hidden glances from one another.

Amid such delight, I suffered alone
and this embittered the pain that I felt.
Watching those lovers, each one with his own,

I thought of the days when the two of us dwelled

ardent in love. It nearly cost me my life
before that could be: I plead and I wheeled

before I could win you to clasp as my wife!
In anger you've all but severed those ties
and now, not having composed our strife,

I've been summoned into this wilderness.
Not even Inao, who bore the curved blade,
when parted from Chindra knew sorrow like this; *hi'sso special*

or Sudhan, Manohra gone from his side;
not Rama when Sita was stolen from him.
Not even to Indra the Thousand-Eyed,

did such heartache as mine, such anguish, come
the time his lady took her love to the grave.
Though masters of the earth, the four of them

were humbled by Love and brought to grief.
Yet even their woes weighed far less than mine:
not one month had passed since you rebuffed me,

and my friends were already noting how thin
my body had grown, reduced to its frame;
I wouldn't say why. So, over the scene ⌣ *it's bc you not wnt*

in that place of smooth currents, Pleasant Stream,
in these long thoughts absorbed, I gazed—until
the sun neared his setting. Then by the way I came,

I turned back to our campsite beside the Hill.

A local waterway, Copper River becomes known as Pleasant River near the Buddha's Footprint, where it flows past a palace, now ruined, constructed by King Prasatong (r. 1630-1655) for use during pilgrimages.

The court women who appear in "Aubade with Elephants" and "The Cave-that-is-Screened" return in this passage—with their bad luck. Watching them interact with the male attendants in this idyllic pastoral setting, Phu once more demonstrates his knowledge of Thai literature and drama by referencing several analogous cases in which men were separated from their wives: Inao, from the romance of the same name, who is summoned to war; Prince Sudhan, who through the connivance of a vizier is sent away from court while his wife, the bird-woman Manohra, is threatened with execution; Rama of the *Ramayana*, whose wife is abducted from him and attempts suicide ("Sita hanging herself in the theater"); and the god Indra, whose wife died for shame after having been violated by a demon disguised as the god.

Phu alternates between the melancholic voice of the *nirat* and genuine delight at this *amoenus locus*. The setting, however, is so idealized that we only half-believe it exists; as at Chalawan Cave, Phu's narrative blurs the line between real and fantastic.

Plays & Punches

At camp I saw friends, once near and dear,
but shied from their company, and from their questions—
in my heart wanting nothing more than to hear

His Highness, the gods' kinsman, announce
when to the sanctuary we would return
of Bell Temple. I'd take my leave at once

and see you again. For this, how I burned!
The next day, the Minister of Finance,
looking for still more merit to earn,

festooned a *sala* for a performance
of *The Swan Prince*. Fairgoers crowded around
to see this old tale enacted in dance

in time to the wooden clappers' clear sound.
That morning, the Swan Prince lost his kite
and, after searching for it, a princess found

concealed in a tower, upon which height
her handmaid then fixed an enchanted spear.
By afternoon, its poisoned point had pierced his side.

The countryfolk watching burst into tears;
at least, those not embroiled in their own chatter.
After the drama ended, the boxers appeared

in two lines, each man facing his contender.
With white bands bound to their heads for good luck,
not one man had the least fear of the other.

As they called out the rounds, great blows were struck
—kneecaps to stomachs, heels flying to foreheads—
and face-crossing forearms bore the full shock

of elbows and fists. From side to side
the fighters would weave until a man went down,
and then what a roar uprose from the crowd!

Large sums were awarded to those who won

for black eyes, broken lips, noses that bled.
Even I lost myself in the fun to be had.

§

Even in Thailand today, no temple fair is complete without traditional entertainment like classical dance-drama or *muay thai* kickboxing. The hosts who sponsor such events believe they earn spiritual merit for these spectacles.

While Thai kickboxing hardly needs an introduction these days, *lakhon nok* is a type of dance-drama characterized by all-male casts, bawdy, often extemporized humor, and storylines drawn from the Jataka tales, a collection of Buddhist folklore. The poem tells us what we need to know about *Suphannahong* (literally "the golden swan"), the protagonist of the play performed here, who possesses a mechanical flying swan, dies for love, and is later revived.

Epilogue

The Sage, who through great striving won Release,
this hilltop with his foot hath sanctified,
which my good fortune was to see and twice

each day to circle with his chapel on my right.
In all, four days drew out their length until
His Highness, born of heaven, bid

our company return unto his temple walls.
The following dawn, the waning moon's third,
before the Buddha's Print we bowed farewell.

At Landing we made no camp, but aboard
the fleet cast off from shore—I, more than all, eager
to be reunited with my adored.

But only my body was born on the river;
my heart had returned to you long before.
In a day and a half we reached city and cloister

where, spending the night, my pain started to clear.
I've composed this *nirat* so as to record
the ills I've endured in this Year of the Hare

(what was of no interest I left from these words).
If you've not made this trip, then read with care.
With you who do, or you by whom these *Poems* are heard,

a portion of the merit made I'll share.

77

§

Phu left for the Buddha's Footprint with the royal corps on "the twelfth [day]/the moon had grown" and arrives to see the Temple illuminated by the full moon in its splendor. He leaves for Bangkok after the moon has waned for three evenings—on Valentine's morning, 1807, "eager/to be reunited" with his own Moon, the lady Chan. But only ostensibly is his *nirat* addressed to her; it's clear that Phu imagined a much wider readership. And for those of us who have followed Phu's journey from beginning to end, the poet offers his blessing.

Poems from the Buddha's Footprint:
A Guide

Almost ninety miles north of Bangkok lies one of Thailand's most fabled places of worship, Wat Phra Phutthabaht or the Temple of the Buddha's Footprint. In February 1807, four days before the Magha Puja holiday, members of Bangkok's royal courts set out on pilgrimage for the Footprint, an annual tradition already two centuries old in their time. Among them went high-ranking court officials, sons of the royal family ordained as Buddhist monks, and even a host of palace women hilariously unsuited for the wilderness. Although today the trip takes less than three hours by car, for these pilgrims the Footprint lay three days ahead: the first two by boat, the third on elephant-back.

This motley procession may have been lost to us had it not included in its lower ranks a 21-year old page named Phu (pronounced "pooh"). At the time, he was in the service of Prince Pathamavamsa, then ordained as a Buddhist monk at Wat Rakhang, the Temple of the Bell, directly across the Chao Phraya River from Bangkok's Grand Palace. If, after visiting the Palace, you decide to leave by boat, putting behind you the crowds of tourists and hawkers that throng the streets outside, and wait for the ferry at Maharaj Pier, you can still see it standing across the brown water. Today, the Temple is dwarfed downriver by the spire of Wat Arun, the Temple of the Dawn, and upriver by Siriraj Medical Center, but in Phu's time it would have overlooked this stretch of river, with its piers and wooden shanties, alone. At daybreak Phu would have seen a nearly full moon hanging low behind its spires as he and his fellow servants rowed away from shore.

It was the twelfth day of the Third Month of 2350, a Year of the Rabbit—February 8th, 1807. Europe was embroiled in the Napoleonic wars; in the United States, Lewis and Clark had just traced a route to the Pacific and spanned the new country from sea to sea. And in Siam, as Thailand was then known, it was the twenty-fifth year since King Rama I had ascended the throne and established Bangkok as his capital, and forty since the former capital of Ayutthaya was sacked by the Burmese. Under the monarch's strong and thoughtful rule, however, the kingdom was experiencing a renaissance: the country was at peace, the arts flourishing, and old traditions returning to life—traditions like the pilgrimage to the Buddha's Footprint.

Prince Pathamavamsa was not one of Rama I's children, but the eldest son of the Lord of the Hind Court, a "third king" after the Viceroy or Lord of the Front, and from the monarch himself. Among his servants, Phu was probably neither the most distinguished nor the most fortunate. Although in later years Phu's gift for poetry would bring him rank and honor at court, plus the title by which we know him today—Sunthorn Phu, "Phu the Eloquent," Thailand's most celebrated poet—in early 1807, Phu's fortunes were at an ebb. His wife of barely a year had born a grudge against him since before the New Year, and they had not reconciled before Phu was called away. Chan was her name, "moon," and images of moon-gazing, a standard of romantic poetry the world over, fill the poem that Phu wrote in his absence from her: the *Nirat Phra Baht,* these *Poems from the Buddha's Footprint.*

But this *Nirat Phra Baht* is not a work of private passion. Instead, it was meant to be read and enjoyed by a wider audience, and today is a classic of early Bangkok literature. In it, Phu offers a rare and intimate glimpse into a world bygone today and sequestered in its own time: a royal procession out of Bangkok, past the ruins of Ayutthaya, and into the hills and caves beyond both cities. Phu does this with his typical wit, attention to detail, and self-deprecating humor, all contained in the masterful verse for which he is rightfully called "eloquent."

I. A Poet of Four Reigns

Phu's long and varied life, the stuff of Thai literary legend, is best understood in relation to the four royal courts he lived to serve. Like Shakespeare, however, Phu is a shadowy figure in Thai history, and much of what we believe we know about him is conjecture, based equal parts in tales handed down at court and from statements in his own, presumptively autobiographical, *nirat.*

Phu was born on June 26th, 1786, four years into the reign of King Rama I, to parents who divorced around the same time. Phu's father took holy orders in a provincial town where he became abbot, while Phu's mother remained in Bangkok, where she was a wet nurse to one of the ladies of the Hind Court, who may have been a distant relative. Through this connection Phu secured the court's patronage as a young man and entered Prince Pathamavamsa's service.

The reign of King Rama II (1809-1824) saw Phu's rise to honor. A poet himself, the Second King lavishly supported the arts, especially literature and drama. He assembled at his court a coterie of poets tasked with the creation of new works for his reign, as well as the revision of preexisting ones for performance at court. Among these poets Phu was a favorite, and he was active in composing the long romances and dramas that characterize the literature of the Second Reign. For Phu's service, the monarch raised him to the rank of *Khun*—a middling title of conferred nobility—*Suntharavoharn*, "of the eloquent verses." During this time, Phu is famously supposed to have snubbed the King's eldest son, Crown Prince Jessadabodin, by revising one of his verses before his father and assembled poets. Legend claims that the prince never forgot this insult: though modern scholars doubt the veracity of the tale, upon Jessadabodin's accession as Rama III in 1824, Phu abruptly left the court to become a Buddhist monk.

Phu spent much of the Third Reign in the monkhood. Although he occasionally taught and mentored several young members of the royal family, Phu described this time of his life as one of relative want and itinerancy. Not until the Fourth Reign—that of the famous King Mongkut—and towards the end of his life would Phu fully enter the royal service again. Appointed to the palace where he had served as a young man, Phu maintained records and performed miscellaneous literary tasks like turning palace chronicles into verse and penning lullabies for the royal children. He died in 1856 at the age of seventy and with the elevated rank of *Phra*, the third highest title of non-inherited nobility.

Since his bicentennial in 1986, Phu has been recognized as Thailand's national poet, one honored by the United Nations Educational, Scientific, and Cultural Organization (UNESCO) for his contributions to Thai culture and society. Sunthorn Phu Day now falls on June 26th of each year, when selections from his writing are performed at schools and cultural centers throughout the country. Even excluding his work in the salons of the Second Reign, Phu was a prolific writer, producing a handful of dance-dramas, several *nirat* or travel poems, and the epic-length *Phra Aphaimanee* ("Lord Aphaimanee"), for which he is best known, over his lifetime. For much of that lifetime, however, and especially in the period when *Poems from the Buddha's Footprint* was written, such acclaim could hardly have seemed possible.

In early 1806, the year before his pilgrimage to the Buddha's Footprint, Phu spent several months in prison for courting one of the palace women. In those days the royal palaces of Siam were strictly divided between their "outer" courts, where men of the royal family conducted the business of state, and the domestic "inner" courts privy only to their respective rulers and which housed their wives, concubines, daughters, and maidservants. Phu had an affair with one such maiden, a certain Chan, and both were imprisoned for their transgression.

Upon their release, Phu went to visit his father in the provinces, passing the midyear rains with him before returning to Bangkok to marry Chan. By this time, the Lord of the Hind Court had passed away, and one of his queens apparently consented to the match. How blissful their married life was, however, we can only imagine: by early 1807 Chan was already not speaking to her husband: "Ever since the Second Month, you nursed a grudge against me," Phu writes in the prologue to the *Poems*. Throughout the *nirat*, Phu also alludes to the existence of other suitors for Chan's hand and sues time and again for her fidelity. While the reasons for Chan's rancor are unknown, tradition holds that Phu was a heavy drinker, and that this drove a wedge between them. What's certain is that the two eventually separated, Chan leaving Phu with their son—but not before the poet had commemorated her as his "Moon" in verse.

II. The Buddha, Gods, and Spirits: The Spiritual Landscape of *Nirat Phra Baht*

Phu understood the vicissitudes of his life through the lenses of two Buddhist concepts: that all phenomena is in constant flux and that human affairs are bound to the immutable law of karma.

The route to the Buddha's Footprint gives Phu several places in which to reflect on *anicha*, the impermanence that the Buddha taught is characteristic of existence and one of the primary reasons why clinging to the body and other material things is an inherent source of suffering. Phu sees *anicha* all around him: in the changing of place-names over time, in rivers that break into branches, and especially at the ruins of Ayutthaya. Phu was born fifteen years after Burmese forces razed the city, and the memory of that once-splendid capital was still fresh among Bangkokians of the time: "By my grandparents I have been told," Phu writes, "that, once before, Ayutthaya prospered... " The rise and fall of empires touches Phu because of what it suggests about the inner life of human beings: that feelings, even love itself, are subject to transience.

Praying before the Buddha's Footprint, Phu claims he was born "to poor karma in this lifetime." Karma literally means "action," and refers to the idea that as one sows, one reaps. Acts of volition bring with them positive or negative consequences based on the integrity of those acts. In Phu's worldview, the troubles he suffers are thus the result of past misdeeds, which can dog a person through several reincarnations until a moral debt is paid. Good karma, and therefore a more comfortable rebirth, is earned by following the *sila,* or Buddhist code of conduct: through acts of charity and kindness; through purging the mind of anger and attachment; and by paying homage to sacred objects and sites like the Buddha's Footprint.

Certain pre-Buddhist beliefs also underlie the worldview of Phu's society. Several times in the poem, Phu refers to the existence of spirits. He enlists their aid for comfort and protection: half-jokingly at Spoke Village, which he imagines as "Spook Village," and more seriously at the shrine on Fallen Hill: "Before those idols I lit candles and prayed/that in the jungle's lap they'd keep us safe." Equally prevalent as this animism are elements from Hinduism. The Hindu gods—especially Vishnu, Brahma, and Indra—figure largely in the Buddhist mythology of Thailand and neighboring countries. This is a legacy of the region's Brahmanistic past and the monarch's traditional identification with these figures. They even decorate the door panels at the Buddha's Footprint. But while worshipping these beings may bring about material benefits, in Phu's cosmology even gods and spirits are subject to the laws of impermanence and karma. Only the Buddha has transcended them.

III. The Buddha's Footprint

Early Buddhist art was aniconic; that is, no anthropomorphic representations of the Buddha were made during the early centuries of his religion. Instead, we find various objects in place of the Buddha's person, namely the Pho tree (*Ficus religiosa*), under which the Buddha gained Enlightenment; the eight-spoked Wheel, representing his ministry; the three Gemstones of the Buddha, the Dharma (his teaching), and the Sangha (clergy); and the pervasive image of his footprint.

There are several explanations for why the footprint is so significant in Buddhist iconography. One is the abundance of metaphors likening Buddhist practice to a path. The Buddha taught the Middle Way, a path between the physical austerities undertaken by ascetics of his day and a life of hedonism, and the Eightfold Path of skills and qualities an individual must cultivate to reach Enlightenment. One of the most widely-read books in the Buddhist canon is the *Dhammapada*, wherein the suffix *-pad* ("foot") implies both a metrical foot as well as a path to follow. However, the significance of the footprint may ultimately have its roots in one of a Buddhist monk's most basic activities: the alms-round, when monks walk from house to house to receive offerings of food and toiletries.

Rock formations resembling footprints are therefore natural objects of veneration in Buddhist countries. Several such places exist in Asia, most famously atop Adam's Peak in Sri Lanka. In Thailand, the Buddha's Footprint sits on a hill in Saraburi province, some eighty miles north of Bangkok, and was discovered in the early seventeenth century. According to legend, a hunter came across the Print while tracking a deer that emerged from a thicket miraculously healed of an arrow-wound. Sunken into the rock beneath the foliage was an impression the length of his arm and shaped like a human foot. Drinking the water inside, the huntsman was cured of a chronic skin ailment. Upon learning of this, the monarch of the time erected a shrine on the spot and built roads and wayside shelters leading to what was immediately recognized as a Buddha's Footprint.

The account of a French delegate to Ayutthaya in 1687 closely corroborates the traditional date of the Temple's founding. Appointed by King Louis XIV as his "Envoy Extraordinaire" to Siam, Simon de la Loubere's *De Royaume du Siam* describes both the Buddha's Footprint and the awe in which it was held:

> The Siamese adore it, and are persuaded that the elephants,
> especially the white ones, the rhinoceros, and all the other beasts of
> their woods, do likewise go to worship it when no person is there;
> and the King of Siam himself goes to adore it once a year with a
> great deal of pomp and ceremony. It is covered with a plate of
> gold, and enclosed in a chapel which is there built.

This tradition of royal patronage and pilgrimage by Thais from all walks of life continues to the present day. Popular belief holds that anyone who worships at the Print once a year for nine consecutive years wins rebirth in heaven, probably because, for most of its history, even one trip to the Footprint was a feat. In Phu's time it was surrounded by dense jungle teeming with tigers and bandits, both of which Phu mentions. This inaccessibility, no doubt, enhanced the Temple's mystique over the centuries, and it remains virtually unchanged today.

IV. *Nirat*: Poems of Place

In Thai literature, *nirat* are travel poems, records of journeys taken away from, and addressed to, an absent lover. In addition to straightforward travel narrative, they employ one major poetic convention: a constant wordplay or metaphor-making that ties features of the passing landscape, local plants and animals, and the names and histories of human habitations to the speaker's emotional state or to thoughts of the beloved. In this way, *nirat* transcend the specificities of particular locales to map not only physical topographies, but also the landscape of the heart. Thus, when Phu encounters "part" palms, he thinks of "parting"; at the monastery Our Lady of Woes, he "could only [his] lady remember." At Fallen Hill, he thinks of his sunken fortunes; at Cleft Hill, how he and Chan have been "cleft in twain." Even the title of this work as a whole has double meanings: on one level, *Nirat Phra Baht* means the *"nirat* of His Highness." But the word *phra baht* literally means the "foot" of an esteemed personage, the only part of such a being that lowlier creatures may address. Thus, *Nirat Phra Baht* refers simultaneously to the leader of Phu's expedition and to its destination, the Buddha's Footprint.

Phu was not only a prolific writer of *nirat* poems, but established its form and conventions for later generations of Thai poets. It was he who popularized the use of the long and continuous *klon* meter for these works, instead of knitting together shorter stanzaic forms with their constant stop-and-go motion. Under Phu, the *nirat* gained expression as a truly narrative form, able to encompass long and detailed accounts of the journeys, both external and internal, they describe.

V. The Translation

The urge to translate Phu's *nirat* came to me while in high school, when I first encountered excerpts from the poems on a Thai literature website. Much of Phu's language was beyond me at the time, but not his music, and one line in particular remained with me for many years: (*phruksa suan luan dai ru-doo dok*), "the orchard flora had all reached the hour of bloom." There is in this single line an interweaving of alliterative sounds that unfolds over the eight syllables, plus the special internal rhyme ("*suan*" and "*luan*") characteristic of Phu's work. Phu was a master of this eight-syllable *klon,* and his simplest lines bear this aural signature. For a verse form originally meant to be chanted or sung, this richness of sound is essential.

When I first tried translating Phu as an undergraduate, I avoided not only replicating this complicated form, but the use of rhyme altogether. Although rhyme is an essential part of Thai verse in general and of Phu's in particular, the pronounced rhythms of English rhymed verse seemed inhospitable to the anglicized names of Thai temples and villages. Furthermore, I couldn't at that time envision rhyming my way through hundreds of lines of solid verse—which, in any case, would be hopelessly old-fashioned, or so I was often led to believe. However, even then I felt that free verse would misrepresent Phu's work, and only a regular, regulated form could properly suggest his style. The question was: which?

At the time, I had been immersed in Robert Fitzgerald's translations of Homer and Virgil. It was his *Odyssey* in 11th-grade English that formally introduced me to the idea of translation as art, shaping my nascent yearnings from high school, and I modeled my initial translations of Phu after Fitzgerald's loose blank verse:

> A sorry turn of fate: to have a love
> And yet, unable to remain with her,
> I must forsake my heart far out of sight.

I finished less than five pages in this vein before growing bored and frustrated. To my ears, these early attempts seemed to lack the elegance I saw in Phu. Most of all, I think I was missing the music of rhyme.

I made no more serious attempts to translate Phu until graduate school. Initially I was just experimenting; I had been reading Laurence Binyon's terza rima translation of the *Inferno* and wondered how a translation out of Thai would sound in that form. I had never considered terza rima a viable option before, since it demands not just paired, but triple rhymes, but scribbled a few lines anyway, figuring it could prove instructive. In the end, I finished my entire translation of the *Poems* in terza rima for the reason with which all literary translators must justify their decisions: it worked. In terza rima, I found a form created for conveying long, continuous narrative, and one impelled by an interlocking series of rhymes analogous to the *klon's*. Allowing myself to use slant and near rhyme only added to the sense of freedom-in-chains that Dante's stanza afforded me.

Despite being Thailand's foremost classical poet, few translations of Sunthorn Phu have been made into English, and all are virtually obscure even inside Thailand. Most were commissioned by the Thai government to mark his bicentennial in 1986, and often read with the elegance of a legal document. Although the late Montri Umavijani, to whom the task of translation mostly fell, was a respected scholar bilingual in Thai and English and a competent poet in both languages, his translations of Phu are uncharacteristically stiff and awkward. This is most apparent in his selections from *Nirat Phra Baht* from *Sunthorn Phu: An Anthology;* The Office of National Culture Commission, 1990, which covers mainly the start of his journey, Ayutthaya, and the celebrations at the Buddha's Footprint. See how Umavijani renders Phu contemplating the moon (page 39, lines unnumbered):

> I look up at the moon:
> The moon travels in the sky.
> Seeing the moon makes me think of you.
> My sorrow is too great to describe poetically.

Apparently. Or Phu's dream of his wife: "Some warmth makes me doze off. / No doubt I dream of love...The dream makes me quite happy" (44). This is Phu drained off all pathos and cast in English so serviceable, so undeniably "accurate," even a civil servant's sensibilities would not be offended. Just as practical is Umavijani's decision to transliterate the names of all places encountered by Phu, even where the poet puns on them, and to rely on footnotes to explain Phu's wordplay. For instance, Umavijani translates (34-35):

> At the crosswise canal of Bang Chak, I grow sad.
> Whoever named the district thus to bar my way
> As if the name might take away my love?

The gloss to this passage explains that "the name suggests separation or bereavement". While these transliterations serve a utilitarian purpose, making the various localities identifiable on a map of Thailand, they interrupt the flow of narrative and detract from an English reader's ability to engage with Phu's wordplay.

In my own translation, where knowledge of a proper name's literal meaning is essential to understanding a pun or simile, I invent English approximations: Khao Khad is, for example, "Cleft Hill," the "great" or "regal" village of Bang Luang, "Crownton." These creative licenses were made to facilitate the reader's appreciation of the text without recourse to glosses and to demonstrate something of the wit that went into Phu's wordplay. Finally, although Phu wrote one long, continuous poem, I have broken his *nirat* into individual poems, each followed by relevant information, so that his work can be enjoyed in manageable units. This was also a practical decision as a writer; it allowed me to pause occasionally and "reset" the demanding rhyme scheme, starting over now and again at Rhyme A.

At the end of his long travel poem, Phu expresses the wish that those who have never seen the Buddha's Footprint will read his work carefully. With them, he says, he'll share a portion of the merit he made while worshipping there. Thus, Phu intended that his poem serve as not only a source of pleasure and information for his audience, but be a benediction. Now, with this translation, let me double Phu's blessing by adding my own.

Noh Anothai
Chiang Rai, Thailand
August 2016

About the Translator

Noh Anothai was a researcher in languages and literature with the Thailand-United States Education Foundation (Fulbright Thailand) from 2012-13, when he began seriously translating Thai poetry. Since then, his translations and original works have appeared in numerous journals in the U.S. and abroad, including *Words Without Borders*, *Asymptote*, *Tin House*, *Ecotone*, and others. He has also lectured on the translation of Sunthorn Phu for the Siam Society and the Center for Translation Studies at Chulalongkorn University, both in Bangkok. He is currently based in Chiang Rai, Thailand.

47478659R00059

Made in the USA
Columbia, SC
02 January 2019